Dr Stephanie Coker is a barrister at FOURTEEN, a leading Family Law Chambers in London. She has a private family practice dealing with financial remedies following the breakdown of a marriage, as well as unmarried couples. She also advises on complex domestic and international private children matters and civil remedies following domestic abuse. She was called to the Bar in 2015 (Inner Temple). Stephanie undertook her PhD in the area of family law. Alongside practice, she has taught family law, property law and foundations of property at the University of Kent.

# A Practical Guide to Non-Molestation Orders and Occupation Orders in Family Proceedings

# A Practical Guide to Non-Molestation Orders and Occupation Orders in Family Proceedings

Dr Stephanie Coker
Barrister, FOURTEEN
LLB (Hons), LLM, DPhil

Law Brief Publishing

© Stephanie Coker

All rights reserved. No part of this publication may be reproduced, stored in a retrieval system, or transmitted, in any form or by any means, electronic, mechanical, photocopying, recording or otherwise, without the prior permission of the publisher.

Excerpts from judgments and statutes are Crown copyright. Any Crown Copyright material is reproduced with the permission of the Controller of OPSI and the King's Printer for Scotland. Some quotations may be licensed under the terms of the Open Government Licence (http://www.nationalarchives.gov.uk/doc/open-government-licence/version/3).

Cover image © iStockphoto.com/matejmm

The information in this book was believed to be correct at the time of writing. All content is for information purposes only and is not intended as legal advice. No liability is accepted by either the publisher or author for any errors or omissions (whether negligent or not) that it may contain. Professional advice should always be obtained before applying any information to particular circumstances.

Published 2024 by Law Brief Publishing, an imprint of Law Brief Publishing Ltd
30 The Parks
Minehead
Somerset
TA24 8BT

www.lawbriefpublishing.com

Paperback: 978-1-914608-93-3

# PREFACE

Domestic abuse is a significant social problem, which can have detrimental impacts on an individual's health, safety, and wellbeing, as well as to children. In such instances, it may be necessary for legal intervention to protect victims and those affected by such abusive behaviour. One legal response can be through the criminal justice system. For example, the enactment of the Domestic Abuse Act 2021 ('DAA 2021') introduced remedies that are available to protect applicants albeit in a criminal law context. Victims of abuse can also seek civil remedies. Since the 1970s, there have been a range of civil law remedies available for victims of domestic abuse. The current provisions are provided in Part IV of the Family Law Act 1996 ('FLA 1996'), as amended by the Domestic Violence Crime and Victims Act 2004.

The main civil remedies for victims of domestic abuse are non-molestation and occupation orders. A non-molestation order, also known as an injunction, is appropriate and available in circumstances where the applicant seeks to control unwanted behaviour by the respondent and prevent them from acting in a way which is abusive. An occupation order regulates how the parties occupy the property. Occupation orders under the FLA take the form of declaratory orders, which declare the interests in the family home, and regulatory orders, which regulate who occupies the family home. Both orders are commonly sought in family law proceedings and shall be the focus of this book.

This book provides detailed analysis and practical guidance on how to apply for a non-molestation order and occupation orders in family law proceedings under the FLA 1996. Part IV of the FLA 1996 sets out the law relating to the occupation of the family home, domestic violence, and related matters. The relevant procedural rules are to be found in Part 10 of the Family Procedure Rules 2010, supplemented by Practice Direction 10A. This book discusses the general principles, practice, and procedure for family law practitioners, and litigants who may find themselves making or resisting an application for non-molestation and occupation orders. To assist in making or resisting applications, the book considers the court's general approach to the making of non-molestation orders and occupation orders in family law proceedings. It is acknowledged that these orders may also be sought in parallel Children Act proceedings. Whilst Children Act proceedings are not the focus of this book, it provides insight into how to case management these cases in light of the court's application of Practice Direction 12J of the Family Procedure Rules 2010.

Crucially, this provides a helpful toolkit for practitioners based on judicial commentary from judgments as to how to practically manage applications for non-molestation orders and occupation orders. It also looks at the options available to the Court to dispose of these applications such by way of undertakings.

The law is accurate as of 1 October 2023.

*Stephanie Coker*
*November 2023*

# CONTENTS

| | | |
|---|---|---|
| Chapter One | Non-Molestation Orders | 1 |
| 1.1. | What is Molestation? | 1 |
| 1.2. | What is a Non-molestation Order? | 4 |
| 1.3. | Who may apply for a Non-molestation order? | 9 |
| 1.4. | The statutory test for a Non-molestation Order | 12 |
| 1.5. | Duration of Non-molestation Orders | 14 |
| Chapter Two | Non-Molestation Orders Against Minors and Those Lacking Capacity | 17 |
| Chapter Three | Occupation Orders | 23 |
| 3.1. | What is an Occupation Order? | 23 |
| 3.2. | Section 33 Occupation Orders | 24 |
| 3.3. | Section 35 - Occupation Orders | 31 |
| 3.4. | Occupation Orders – section 36 FLA 1996 | 34 |
| 3.5. | Power of Arrest and Occupation Orders | 35 |
| 3.6. | Additional Orders – Provisions for repairs and payment of outgoings | 37 |
| Chapter Four | Without Notice (Ex Parte) Applications | 39 |
| 4.1. | Guidance from case law | 40 |
| 4.2. | Practical tips – The Application and Statements | 43 |
| 4.3. | Duties that attach to ex parte applications | 44 |
| 4.4. | Return Date | 46 |
| 4.5. | Case management | 48 |

| Chapter Five | Undertakings | 51 |
|---|---|---|
| 5.1. | When will the court not accept an undertaking? | 52 |
| 5.2. | Undertakings from respondents aged less than 18 or lacking capacity | 52 |
| 5.3. | Procedural points in connection with undertakings | 53 |
| Chapter Six | Procedural Guidance: Applications for Non-Molestation Orders and Occupation Orders | 55 |
| 6.1. | Making an application | 55 |
| 6.2. | Service of the application and order on the respondent | 56 |
| 6.3. | Service of the order on the Police | 58 |
| 6.4. | Vulnerable persons and Special measures | 59 |
| Concluding Remarks | | 61 |

# CHAPTER ONE

# NON-MOLESTATION ORDERS

## 1.1 What is Molestation?

'Molestation' is not defined in the Family Law Act 1996 ('FLA 1996'). In *Vaughan v Vaughan* [1973] 1 WLR 1159, CA the Court considered the meaning of molestation as synonymous with the word 'pester' which includes behaviour 'to cause trouble; to vex; to annoy; to put to inconvenience'. The definition also includes conduct which does not amount to violent behaviour.[1] In *Horner v Horner* [1983] 4 FLR 50 Ormerod LJ said that molesting 'does not imply necessarily either violence or threats of violence. It applies to any conduct which can properly be regarded as such a degree of harassment as to call for the intervention of the Court'.[2]

Noting that there is no legal definition of 'molestation', in *C v C (Non-molestation Order: Jurisdiction)* [1998] 1 FLR 554, Sir Stephen Brown stated that molestation, 'implies some quite deliberate conduct which is aimed at a high degree of harassment of the other party, so as to justify the intervention of the court'. Lady Justice Hale (as she then was) gave some further assistance in *C v C* [2001] EWCA Civ 1625 when she deemed a non-molestation order justified in circumstances where the conduct complained of 'was calculated to cause alarm and distress to the mother', and 'that is the sort of behaviour, in my

---

[1] *Davis v Johnson* [1979] AC 264 334, HL

[2] See page 51 G.

judgment, which does call for the intervention of the court'. In *Re T (A Child) (Non-molestation Order)* [2017] EWCA Civ 1889, [2018] 1 FLR 1457 at [42]:

> When determining whether or not particular conduct is sufficient to justify granting a non-molestation order, the primary focus, as established in the consistent approach of earlier authority, is upon the 'harassment' or 'alarm and distress' caused to those on the receiving end. It must be conduct of 'such a degree of harassment as to call for the intervention of the court (*Horner v Horner* (1983) 4 FLR 50 and *C v C (Non-Molestation Order: Jurisdiction)* [1998] 1 FLR 554).

Domestic abuse and other abusive behaviours have also been found to amount to molestation. Our understanding of the term 'domestic abuse' has evolved over the years to include a wide range of behaviours. Its most comprehensive definition is found in Practice Direction 12J Family Procedure Rules 2010 ('FPR 2010') as including:

> *'domestic abuse' includes any incident or pattern of incidents of controlling, coercive or threatening behaviour, violence, or abuse between those aged 16 or over who are or have been intimate partners or family members regardless of gender or sexuality. This can encompass but is not limited to psychological, psychological, sexual, financial, or emotional abuse. Domestic abuse also includes culturally specific forms of abuse including, but not limited to, forced marriage, honour-based violence, dowry-related abuse, and transitional marriage abandonment.*[3]

---

[3] FPR 2010, PD12J para 3.

The introduction of the Domestic Abuse Act 2021 provided a broad-ranging definition of domestic abuse on statutory footing. Section 1(3) of the DAA 2021 defines behaviour as abusive 'if it consists of any of the following such as physical or sexual abuse, violent or threatening behaviour, controlling or coercive behaviour, economic abuse, psychological, emotional or other abuse and it does not matter whether the behaviour consists of a single incident or a course of conduct'. It is submitted that this definition can now assist the judges, who have a wide discretion to consider the particulars facts of a case and determine whether molestation is made out.

Does making repeated allegations against another party, which are disputed amount to harassment, such that a non-molestation order is justified? This was considered in *A v B* [2023] EWFC 74, which was a private Children Act application whereby the father initially applied for an order formalising the living arrangements and to limit the mother's spending time arrangements to supervised contact. The mother cross-applied and accused the father of coercive and controlling behaviour and alleged that her suicide attempts had been a response to his conduct. The mother made further allegations against the father. The father then applied for a non-molestation order against the mother for her to be injuncted against making false allegations of abuse against him. His case was that her allegations amounted to harassment. The mother contested the allegations, and thus, the Family Law proceedings were consolidated with the Children Act application.

The court noted that the father had been deeply affronted by what the mother had alleged. However, the judge was not satisfied that by the mother making allegations or raising issues within the proceedings about his conduct, and then not pursuing it, was by itself evidence that the allegations were fabricated or that their initial report was malicious. It followed that the judge was not satisfied that the mother sought to harass him or pester him or otherwise engage in conduct that would call into question the need for a non-molestation order. Practically, the implication of this decision is that respondents should not automatically jump the gun and conclude that a failure to seek findings on allegations implies that they are fabricated. Whilst respondents are likely to feel aggrieved and be keen to refute allegations of domestic abuse, they should bear in mind that the making of allegations in of themselves do not amount to molestation.

In *DS v AC* [2023] EWFC 46, Mrs Justice Lieven stated at [27] that:

> *The law is clear that there does not have to be a positive intent to molest. However, that does not mean that the test is a wholly subjective one whereby the Applicant simply has to feel distress. Such subjective distress does not alone justify the making of an order. The conduct has to be of a nature or degree that justifies the intervention of the court.*

Based on the above, it is submitted that any applicant who can demonstrate evidence of any of the behaviours above can qualify for a non-molestation order. Indeed, in *C v C* [2001] EWCA Civ 1625, Lady Justice Hale (as she then was) held that granting a non-molestation order was justified in circumstances where the conduct complained of "was calculated to cause alarm and distress to the mother".

## 1.2 What is a Non-molestation Order?

Victims of molestation or domestic abuse, in its many and varied forms, are entitled to protection of the Court through the grant of injunctions under Part 4 of the FLA 1996. One of the aims of the FLA 1996 is to protect a victim from conduct amounting to violence, intimidation, harassment, pestering or interference which is sufficiently serious to warrant the intervention of the Court. This is achieved through non-molestation orders. These orders are routinely made to protect applicants from all forms of 'domestic abuse'. A non-molestation order is a protective order containing provisions that prohibit a respondent from molesting another person who is associated with the respondent, and/or prohibiting the respondent from molesting a relevant child.[4] The order aims to prohibit the respondent from inflicting or carrying out some of the conduct listed below.

The non-molestation order can also be made to prohibit the respondent from molesting a relevant child.[5] A 'relevant child' is defined in section 62(2) of the FLA 1996 as any child who is living with or might reasonably be expected to live with either party to the proceedings; or any child to whom an order under the Adoption Act 1976, Adoption and Children Act 2002 or the Children Act 1989 is in question in the proceedings; and any other child whose interests the Court considers relevant.

All non-molestation orders are made under section 42 of the FLA 1996 and is a civil remedy. Although a non-molestation order is a civil remedy, breaching this order without reasonable excuse is a criminal offence under section 42A of the FLA 1996. It follows that a power of arrest does not need to be attached to a non-molestation order. Where a person is convicted of an offence under section 42A that conduct is not punishable as a contempt of court.[6] A person that is convicted of such offence is liable (a) on conviction on indictment to imprisonment

---

[4]  Family Law Act 1996, section 42(1).

[5]  Family Law Act 1996, section 42 (1)(b).

[6]  Family Law Act 1996, section 42A(3).

for a term not exceeding five years, or a fine, or both. On summary conviction, a person convicted is liable to imprisonment for a term not exceeding 12 months, or a fine, or not exceeding the statutory maximum, or both. In the case of a non-molestation order made without notice to a respondent, a person can only be guilty of an offence if they engage in conduct at a time when they were aware that the non-molestation order was in place. Therefore, it is important to ensure that the respondent is served. The procedural requirements regarding service are considered in further detail in Chapter 6.

The FLA 1996 provides that a non-molestation order may be expressed in general terms, or may refer to particular acts of molestation, or to both.[7] The terms of a non-molestation order are often formulaic and commonly include prohibiting the respondent from doing as follows:

(a) Use or threaten any violence towards the applicant.

(b) Come within 100 metres of the applicant's address or any address where the respondent knows the applicant to be living.

(c) Communicate with the applicant whether directly or indirectly, whether orally, by telephone, text message, email, social media, or any other means except through their solicitors.

(d) Threaten the applicant.

---

[7] FLA 1996, section 42(6).

(e) Post any derogatory, insulting, threatening, or harassing posts regarding the applicant on any social media platform.

(f) Not to damage or threaten to damage any property owned by the applicant.

Non-molestation orders can also contain a term prohibiting the respondent from encouraging a third party to do what s/he is prohibited from doing. Clause (b) is an example of a zonal clause as it has the effect of excluding the respondent from attending or coming near a particular address. Careful thought should be given to respondent's that have to come within 100 metres of the applicant's address for good reason. For example, it may be that the respondent has family on that street that he/she regularly visits or has a surgery or dentist for example, within that radius. In such circumstances, respondent's and/or those representing them should consider what practical restrictions may arise with the proposed terms of an order. This can help avoid the respondent being found to have breached the non-molestation order.

In instances where the respondent has a need to enter the street that the applicant lives, it may be worth drafting the order prohibiting the respondent from entering or attempting to enter the specific address. The President's Guidance on non-molestation orders states that "if the court decides to exclude the respondent from a geographical area, the order should specify a named road or roads or a clearly defined area and avoid the use of expressions such as '100 metres from the applicant's home'. The use of maps, which can become detached, should likewise be avoided unless they are embedded into the body of the order".[8]

---

[8] para 18.

A provision prohibiting the respondent from attending a particular address or area could be expressed as a part of an occupation order. However, it is not necessary to make an occupation order for this purpose alone. It is submitted that a provision requiring the respondent to stay away should not be included in a non-molestation order as a matter of routine, but its inclusion must be proportionate and necessary and supported by evidence. This was confirmed by the court in *Mr R v Mrs R* [2014] EWFC 48 wherein Jackson J (as he then was) noted that "extra injunctive provisions such as exclusion areas and orders prohibiting any direct communication between parties should not be routinely included in non-molestation orders. They are serious infringements of a person's freedom of action and require specific evidence to justify them".

Ultimately, when drafting non-molestation orders, it is important to bear in mind that they should be proportionate to the parties' circumstances. In respect of clause (c), it is likely to be inappropriate to bar all communication between the parties, particularly in circumstances where they share children or are in engaged in divorce, financial remedy or Children Act proceedings. Suitable terms in these instances include allowing the parties to communicate via a dedicated email address (if appropriate) or a Parenting App. Whilst communication via solicitors can be a useful third-party avenue, this should not be the only means as the parties may become litigants in person in the future. Also, communicating solely via solicitors can lead to delays in messages being passed on (in an emergency for instance), as well as increase costs for one or both parties.

In many cases, applicants refer to all the terms and seek for them to be included in the non-molestation order made by the court if the application is granted. Whilst this is commonly done, it is good practice to ensure that the orders made are justified by the behaviour complained of. This was shown in *PF v CF* [2016] EWHC 3117

(Fam), which was an appeal by a husband against a judgment and order of HHJ Murfitt under which following an application by the wife, the judge made a non-molestation order against the husband, and an occupation order in respect of the family home. The first instance judge made a non-molestation order with the standard wording forbidding the husband from using or threatening violence against the wife. The husband was also prohibited from encouraging anyone to do so. However, there was no finding of a use or threat of violence. On appeal, Baker J concluded that the judge 'was inadvertently led into making an order in terms that were not supported by her findings'.[9]

## 1.3 Who may apply for a Non-molestation order?

Any individual may apply for a non-molestation order and would be known as the applicant. An individual under the age of 16 may apply for a non-molestation order and occupation order only with the permission of the court.[10] Permission may be granted by the court if "it is satisfied that the child has sufficient understanding to make the proposed application for the occupation order or non-molestation order".[11] At such a hearing, the court will also consider the need for a litigation friend pursuant to Part 16 Family Procedure Rules 2010.

To make the application, the applicant must be an associated person with the respondent.[12] An 'associated person' is defined in section 62

---

[9] para 39.

[10] Family Law Act 1996, section 43(1).

[11] Family Law Act 1996, section 43 (2).

[12] Family Law Act 1996, section 42(2)(a).

of the Family Law Act 1996 and includes circumstances whereby the applicant is or has been:

- married to the respondent

- they are or have been civil partners;

- cohabitants or former cohabitants

- relatives;

- they live or have lived in the same household, other than merely by reason of them being the other's employee, tenant, lodger or boarder;

- they agreed to marry one another (whether or not that agreement has been terminated). In this instance, evidence of agreement to marry is required.

- they have or have had an intimate personal relationship with each other which is or was of significant duration;

- in relation to any child, both are either the parent or has or has had parental responsibility for the child in question;

- they are parties to the same family proceedings (other than proceedings under Part IV of the Family Law Act 1996), an example being under the Children Act 1989.

It will be for the applicant to set out how they are associated with the respondent. This can be satisfied sufficiently in a supporting statement, and by ticking the relevant box in section 4 of the application form titled 'Your relationship with the respondent' below, which is a snapshot of the form.

**4. Your relationship with the respondent**

4.1 If your relationship with the respondent is one of the following, select the one which best describes your relationship and go to question 4.2.

☐ Married or in a civil partnership
☐ Formerly married or in a civil partnership
☐ Engaged or proposed civil partnership
☐ Formerly engaged or proposed civil partnership
☐ Live together as a couple
☐ Formerly lived together as a couple
☐ Boyfriend, girlfriend or partner who does not live with me
☐ Former boyfriend, girlfriend or partner who did not live with me

☐ None of the above. **Go to question 4.4**

4.2 When did your relationship start and when did it end?
Start
Day   Month   Year

**Note 4:** To get an injunction against the respondent, you will need to show the court that you have a connection to them. The courts call this being an 'associated person'.

The questions in this section are used to decide if you are an associated person for this application

**Note 4.2:** If you don't know the exact date your relationship started or ended, give your best guess of the month and year.

The scope of who can be categorised as an 'associated person' has been considered in the case law. In *M v D (Family Law Act 1996: Meaning of "Associated Person")* [2021] EWHC 1351 (Fam), the court considered an appeal against the dismissal of a without notice non-molestation order made under section 42 for want of jurisdiction. The case came before MacDonald J in the High Court on the grounds that the appeal raised an important point of principle or practice, namely, the meaning of the term 'associated person'. The respondent was the appellant's 'step-nephew', and it was her case in relation to being an associated person that the respondent was her 'relative'. At first instance, the District Judge was not satisfied on the balance of probabilities that the appellant was associated with the respondent for the purposes of section 62(3)(d). The appeal was dismissed for a number of reasons including that step-nephews are not provided as a category in section 63(1) FLA 1996 in contradistinction to other step-relationships that are expressly listed under section 63(1)(a).

The court also has the power to make a non-molestation order 'if in any family proceedings to which the respondent is a party the court considers that the order should be made for the benefit of any other party to the proceedings or any relevant child even though no such application has been made'.[13] This provision is very important as it gives the court the power to make a non-molestation order in instances where the applicant is not associated with the respondent. The case of *Re T (A Child)* [2017] EWCA Civ 1889, concerned an appeal which considered the extent to which a family court may exercise its jurisdiction to grant an injunction under the FLA 1996 to protect a child who is subject to a full care order. In this case, the court made a non-molestation order to protect carers from the mother in public child law proceedings, in circumstances where the mother and her partner did not accept the validity of the care order and at various times embarked upon serious attempts to abduct the child from her carers.

## 1.4 The statutory test for a Non-molestation Order

The statutory test and the power of the court to make a non-molestation order is set out in section 42(5) FLA 1996. This provision states that in considering whether to make a non-molestation order, and if so, in what manner, the court shall have regard to all the circumstances of the case including the health, safety and wellbeing of the applicant and any relevant child.

---

[13] Family Law Act 1996, section 42(2)(b).

The following three principles, from *C v C (Non-Molestation Order: Jurisdiction)* [1989] 1 FLR 554, FD, should be considered when determining whether to make a non-molestation order:

(1) There must be evidence of molestation;

(2) The applicant (or child) must need protection; and

(3) The judge must be satisfied on the balance of probabilities that judicial intervention is required to control the behaviour of the respondent.

As Lieven J stated in *DS v AC* [2023] EWFC 46, "orders should not be granted where the evidence suggests that there is some upset at the end of a relationship, and little or nothing to suggest the conduct complained of would amount to 'molestation'".[14] It is submitted that the test applies should also be considered when seeking to extend a non-molestation order.

In *Re C3 and C4 (Child Arrangements)* [2019] EWHC B14 (Fam), the applicant father made a Child Arrangements application in respect of his children, and the mother sought an extension or a new non-molestation order on the terms initially made by DJ Khan in July 2016, and extension of the section 91(14) Children Act order. The father's conduct that was originally relied upon by the mother in support of her application for a non-molestation order was described by Keehan J as 'truly appalling' and 'extraordinary'.[15] The non-molestation order was made for a duration of 3 years. However, there had been no new incidents since the order was made, but the applicant now sought to rely upon the respondent's conduct of litigation and

---

[14] para 26.

[15] para 21.

repeated applications to the court in support of her application for an extension. Keehan J concluded that "there is no authority to support the principle that a non-molestation injunction can be made to prevent a parent commencing litigation: that is solely the purpose and objective of s.91(14). Accordingly, I see as matters, there is no legal basis for now making a non-molestation order".[16] He therefore dismissed the application for an extension of the non-molestation order.

## 1.5 Duration of Non-molestation Orders

Pursuant to section 42(7) of the FLA 1996, a non-molestation order may last for a specified period or until further order. The language of section 42(7) might reasonably be interpreted as suggesting that a non-molestation order should have a finite limit in time, ended either at a named or specified point, or at the latest by the making of a 'further order'. However, in *Re B-J (A Child) (Non-Molestation Order: Power of Arrest)* [2001] 1 All ER 235; [2001] Fam 415, the Court of Appeal noted such interpretation as being too restrictive and not representing the intention of Parliament. In giving the leading judgment and dismissing an appeal against the making of a non-molestation order of indefinite duration, Lady Justice Hale (as she then was) stated that:

> A non-molestation order is indeed sometimes, even often, designed to give a breathing space after which the tensions between the parties may settle down so that it is no longer needed. But in other cases, it may appropriate for a much longer period, and it is not helpful to oblige the courts to

---

[16] para 23.

consider whether such cases are "exceptional" or "unusual".

Having cited the legislation and the Law Commission report which had foreshadowed it, Hale LJ went on to say that:

> There are obviously cases, of which this is one, in which the continuing feelings between parties who separated long ago are such that a long term or indefinite order is justified.

It follows that when considering the appropriate duration of an order, and whether there is merit in seeking an extension of its duration, parties should consider whether there are still grounds for the continuation of the order. It may be that the initial concerns and complaints that existed at the outset persist or have exacerbated. In such cases, having the order last for a longer period would be appropriate. However, where there are no new incidents, the court is unlikely to extend the duration of the order. Generally, the court will order that the non-molestation order lasts for 6 or 12 months.

Ultimately, orders should not remain in place for longer than is required. In *Galan v Galan* [1985] FLR 905, the Court of Appeal confirmed that "[n]ormally an order for a short, fixed period will be the appropriate order, if any, for the court to make" and while an order for an indefinite period will not usually be appropriate, "there is nothing in the 1976 Act expressly to limit the discretion of the court as regards the duration of the order".

A non-molestation order may be varied or discharged by the respondent or the person on whose application the order was made. The court may vary or discharge a non-molestation order made by the court under section 42(2)(b) even if no application has been made.

When looking to extend non-molestation orders, parties should provide a statement setting out the reasons why the extension is needed which include clearly involve addressing the criteria that the court would have initially considered when the application for an injunction was made.

# CHAPTER TWO

# NON-MOLESTATION ORDERS AGAINST MINORS AND THOSE LACKING CAPACITY

There are some cases in which it would be inappropriate for the court to grant a non-molestation order. Such cases are where persons are those under 18 and those without capacity, who are said to have a disability. In terms of those without capacity, this was considered in *Wookey v Wookey; Re S (A Minor)* [1991] 3 All ER 365. This case concerned two separate appeals. In *Wookey*, the wife aged 72-year-old sought a non-molestation order against her husband, aged 70, who was suffering from dementia and had been diagnosed with pathological jealousy of his wife. The husband had been admitted into hospital under section 2 of the Mental Health Act 1983. Attempts had been made to dissuade him from returning to the family home, but these were unsuccessful. The husband continued to be abusive and violent to the wife, culminating in an incident where the wife hit the husband with a rolling pin in self-defence.

The husband was further admitted under section 2. His consultant psychiatrist stated that the husband would not be fit to plead if charged with a criminal offence as he was incapable of understanding the nature of an injunction. The wife applied for a non-molestation order and an order preventing the husband from returning to the family home. The orders sought were granted along with a power of arrest attached. The husband, represented by the Official Solicitor, appealed against the order. The issue was whether it was appropriate to grant a non-molestation order against a person who was suffering under a disability, such that the party either could not understand the meaning of the order or the order could not be appropriately enforced by the court. The second appeal concerned an application by a sister against her 15-year-old brother who had been violent to the sister and assaulted her whilst she was pregnant. The trial judge refused the application and did not grant an order. The sister appealed.

On the facts, it was inappropriate for an injunction to be granted in both appeals. However, the Court allowed the appeal in *Wookey* but dismissed *Re S (A Minor)*. For both appeals, the Court noted that the fact of disability was by itself a bar to the making of an injunction against a person with a disability. In regard to mental incapacity, 'the question was whether the person suffering under that disability understood the proceedings and the nature and requirements of the injunction'.[17] The Court of Appeal held that:

> Where the person against whom the injunction was sought was incapable of understanding what he was doing or that it was wrong, an injunction ought not to be granted because he would not be capable of complying with it and the injunction would not have a deterrent effect and, further, any breach by him would not be subject to effective enforcement proceedings since he would have a clear defence to an application for committal to prison for contempt.

It follows that careful consideration should be given before seeking an injunction against a party that lacks capacity. Rather in such circumstances, where the person has a mental disorder which renders them incapable of managing and administering their property and affairs, the court should "adjourn the matter for the attendance of the

---

[17] [1991] 3 All ER 365 at 373G.

Official Solicitor, or alternatively, in the light of the congestion of the county court lists, adjourn the matter generally with liberty to either side to apply".[18] Butler-Sloss LJ stated that the fears of an applicant against a mentally disordered respondent may be addressed by the operation of section 18 of the Mental Health Act 1983.[19]

Turning to the second appeal. There was no doubt that the 15-year-old understood the non-molestation order. The issue on appeal was whether there was an effective means of enforcing the order, and if not, whether the non-molestation order should be made. An injunction may be enforced by way of committal to prison for a period not exceeding two years or by sequestration of property or a fine. Section 9(1) of the Criminal Justice Act 1982 provides the court with the power to detain a person between the age of 17 and 21 for contempt of court. In *R v Selby Justices, ex p Frame* [1991] 2 All ER 344, the court made clear that the power of the court to commit minors for contempt of court was limited to those who have attained the age of 17. Based on this, there was no dispute that the court did not have jurisdiction to commit a 15-year-old to prison.

In comparison, a writ of sequestration may be issued against a minor. However, to obtain permission there must be property capable of sequestration. This is required in addition to refusal or neglect to comply with, or disobedience to an order. There are also associated fees with this procedure such as appointing a sequestrator, their fees which are usually paid out of the property owned by the individual. In this case, the minor had no assets worth seizing. In particular, the court noted that 'in almost all cases concerning minors there will not be the assets available to justify an application for leave to issue the

---

[18] [1991] 3 All ER 365 at 373D-E.

[19] [1991] 3 All ER 365 at 373C.

writ'.[20] This means in principle a writ of sequestration can be considered as an alternative, but this procedure may not be suitable in circumstances where the individual minor does not have property available to justify the issue of the writ.

A fine may be a possibility to enforce a non-molestation order that may be breached by a minor under 18. A fine can be enforced by way of an attachment of earnings order, but not in respect of state benefits.[21] However, for this option to 'bite' the minor should have some income. As stated by the judge, 'in some cases a fine for even a small fine would bite if the income of the minor is small'.[22] Consideration should consider whether the minor has some income. It may be useful to provide evidence regarding the minor's income, no matter how small this may be. In this appeal, the 15-year-old was under school leaving age and there was no evidence that he was earning income at all.

Finally, there may be circumstances whereby an application for a non-molestation order against disobedient teenager in good employment may be warranted. If an order is made, a penal notice must be attached. However, given the points drawn out above, the prescribed wording for a minor to be committed to prison for non-compliance would be unsuitable. The judgment noted that the wording was not mandatory, and with reference to rule 2(2) of the County Court (Forms) Rules 1982, SI 1982/586, there may be varied as the circumstances may require. Here, Butler-Sloss LJ suggested that "a penal notice in the unusual circumstances of a minor under 17, should

---

[20] [1991] 3 All ER 365 at 373H.

[21] Attachment of Earnings Act 1971, section 24(2)(c).

[22] [1991] 3 All ER 365 at 373I.

be adapted by deleting 'you may be sent to prison' and substituting 'you may be fined'".[23]

In sum, in respect of minors "the court should investigate whether it was feasible to enforce the injunction by means of a fine, in which case the penal notice attached to the order should be adapted by substituting the threat of a fine for the threat of imprisonment". Nonetheless, for most cases where a minor is still in school age, or unemployed, recourse to the civil courts is not the appropriate procedure. Consideration should be given to an application by the local authority for care proceedings for children that are beyond parents control, or a compliant to the police of a criminal act.[24]

---

[23] [1991] 3 All ER 365 at 374F.

[24] [1991] 3 All ER 365 at 373G.

# CHAPTER THREE

# OCCUPATION ORDERS

## 3.1 What is an Occupation Order?

An occupation order is a remedy that is available to protect an applicant and/or relevant child from conduct (such as molestation) from the respondent, by regulating the occupation of the family home. Occupation Orders are covered under sections 33 to 38 FLA 1996. The court's powers, the factors that shall be considered in determining whether to make an occupation order, and the maximum duration of occupation orders vary from section to section. Consequently, it is important to carefully consider the provision that is being relied upon and the factors that need to be established to give the court jurisdiction to make an occupation order.

Occupation orders are commonly known to exclude one individual, i.e., the respondent, from the property. However, under each section the court can make orders to regulate the occupation of the home by either or both parties, declare the right of the applicant to remain in occupation of the property, allow the applicant to enter the home if they are excluded, exclude the respondent from the property and vicinity of the home, and to prohibit, terminate or restrict the exercise of the respondent's occupation rights, as appropriate.[25] However, it should be noted that the court has no power to extinguish these occupation rights.

---

[25] Family Law Red Book, s.2.610[1] p.919.

There are five categories of applicants under the FLA 1996 who are eligible to apply for an occupation order. These three categories can be found under sections 33, 35, 36, 37 or 38 of the FLA 1996. Practitioners and parties (where acting in person) will need to check carefully under which section they are bringing their client's application for an occupation order.

## 3.2   Section 33 Occupation Orders

Section 33 is much wider in scope than the other sections dealing with occupation orders. The requirements for an occupation order under section 33 provide as follows: -

(1) If—

    (a) a person ("the person entitled")—

        i. is entitled to occupy a dwelling-house by virtue of a beneficial estate or interest or contract or by virtue of any enactment giving him the right to remain in occupation, or

        ii. has [home rights] in relation to a dwelling-house, and

    (b) the dwelling-house—

        i. is or at any time has been the home of the person entitled and of another person with whom he is associated, or

> ii. was at any time intended by the person entitled and any such other person to be their home,
>
> the person entitled may apply to the court for an order containing any of the provisions specified in subsections (3), (4) and (5).

The above shows that applications under this section can be made if three conditions are satisfied. The first is that the applicant is entitled to occupy. Most applications by spouses will be made under this section as the majority are entitled to occupy by virtue of their interest in the property or they have home rights. Under section 30 of the FLA 1996, where one spouse or civil partner has the right to occupy a dwelling-house, either because they own it or have a contractual tenancy or is a statutory tenant of it, the other party has home rights. If the individual is in occupation of the property, the home rights mean that they cannot be evicted without the permission of the court or, if they are not in occupation, the right to return to the property if they are not in occupation of it.

The second condition is that the respondent is associated with the applicant as defined under section 62(3) of the FLA 1996.[26] This was discussed in detail in chapter 2. The final condition is that the house is, was or was intended to be the home of the applicant and respondent.

Parties who were formerly engaged may also make an application for an occupation order under this section. According to section 33(2), 'if an agreement to marry is terminated, no application under this section may be made by virtue of section 62(3)(e) by reference to that

---

[26] See previous chapters.

agreement after the end of the period of three years beginning with the day on which it is terminated'. In essence, those who are engaged have three years from the day on which the agreement to marry was terminated to make an application under this section. Where the three-year period has lapsed, they are barred from bringing such an application under this provision as the respondent would no longer be considered as associated. A similar position applies where a civil partnership agreement is terminated.[27]

An occupation order made under section 33 of the Act can be varied or discharged by the court on the application by any person deriving title under the other spouse or trustees affected by the charge if the other's home rights are a charge on the estate or interest of the other spouse under section 31. The correct form for the application is FL406. When looking to extend these orders, parties should provide a statement setting out the reasons why the extension is needed which include clearly involve addressing the criteria that the court would have initially considered when the application for an injunction was made.

### 3.2.1 The court's powers under section 33

The court's powers are set out in section 33(3) and include the power to require that the respondent leaves the property. These powers include an order enforcing the applicant's entitlement to remain in occupation over the respondent, require that the respondent permit the applicant to enter and remain in the property or part of it, regulate the occupation of the property by either or both parties, require the

---

[27] FLA 1996, section 3 (2A).

respondent to leave the property or part of it or excluding the respondent from a defined area.

There is no maximum duration for an order under section 33. Subsection 10 states that 'an occupation order made under section 33, in so far as it has continuing effect, may be made for a specified period, until the occurrence of a specified event or until further order'. Whilst there is no maximum duration for an order, in practice, the courts tend to order that they remain in place for 6 months, and this can be extended for a further 6 months. Given how draconian this power is, the courts will be mindful not to exclude an individual from their home unnecessarily or for longer than can be justified.

There have been occasions when the occupation orders have been extended until the conclusion of the final hearing at which point the application is fully determined. This may be appropriate on occasions where findings are yet to be made, and due to delays if the harm likely to be suffered remains a concern such that the respondent should still be excluded. In opposing an extension of an occupation order, a party may wish to address the court on any further harm that they are likely to suffer as a result of the order remaining in place. This may be due to a lack of financial resources or available accommodation amongst other reasons.

### 3.2.2 The relevant criteria to be applied by the court under section 33

The court has a discretionary power when considering an application for an occupation order. In deciding whether to exercise its powers to make an occupation order to achieve either of the aims listed in subsection (3), the FLA 1996 provides the court with two available routes. The first route is via section 33(7) of the FLA 1996, which is known as the 'balance of harm test'. The second route is known as the discretionary criteria under section 33(6) of the Act. In practice, the court will first consider the balance of harm test, and if this cannot be satisfied, then the Court shall move on to consider the discretionary criteria. This was confirmed in *Chalmers v Johns* [1999] 1 FLR 392.

In preparing written evidence and in making oral submissions to the court in such applications, practitioners should address both tests under section 33(7) and (6). From experience, most applications tend to be argued under the discretionary test due to how high the significant harm test threshold appears to be. The term significant harm under this provision has the same meaning as the significant harm threshold under section 31(2) of the Children Act 1989.

### 3.2.3 The balance of harm test

Section 33(7) states as follows:

> If it appears to the Court that the applicant or any relevant child <u>is likely to suffer significant harm</u> attributable to conduct of the respondent if an order under this section containing one or more of the provisions mentioned in subsection (3) is not made, the Court shall make the order unless it appears to it that –
>
> (a) The respondent or any relevant child is likely to suffer significant harm if the order is made; and
>
> (b) <u>The harm likely to be suffered by the respondent or the child in that event is as great as, or greater than, the harm attributable to conduct of the respondent which is likely to be suffered by the applicant or child if the order is not made.</u>

Plainly, the court is considering where the greater harm will lie if an order is made. In *G v G* [2000] 3 FCR 53, the court highlighted that the correct approach to section 33(7) is to assess the effect of the respondent's conduct on the applicant or any relevant child, rather than to focus on the intention of the respondent. In this way, relevant points to draw upon include how the conduct may impact on the applicant's health, safety, and wellbeing as well as that of the child. The court will make an occupation order if it appears that the applicant or relevant child is likely to suffer significant harm as a result of the respondent's behaviour if an order is not made, and the harm is likely to be greater than that suffered by the respondent if an order was not made.

The court is unlikely to make an occupation order under section 33(7) if it appears to it that the respondent or any relevant child is likely to suffer significant harm if the occupation order is made, and the harm suffered by the respondent or child if an order is made <u>is as great as or greater than</u> the harm likely to be suffered by the applicant or relevant child as a result of the respondent's behaviour if an occupation order is not made. If the court is not persuaded under section 33(7), then the applicant (and/or their representatives) should be invited to consider its discretionary powers under subsection 6.

Occupation orders excluding a party with a right to occupy from the property are draconian and should only be granted in 'exceptional circumstances' if there is no significant harm. Respondents who may be faced with an application for an occupation order excluding them from the property may wish to bear this in mind where there is no significant harm. In such instances, a party responding to an application for an occupation order will want to persuade the court that the circumstances are not exceptional and therefore an order should not be made. However, the reality is, that the applicant may revert to subsection 6 and invite the court to make an occupation order under its discretionary criteria.

### 3.2.4 The discretionary criteria – section 33(6)

This is arguably a lower threshold to the significant harm test. Section 33(6) provides that:

> In deciding whether to exercise its powers under subsection (3) and (if so) in what manner, the Court shall have regard to all the circumstances including -
>
> (a) The housing needs and housing resources of each of the parties and of any relevant child;
>
> (b) The financial resources of each of the parties;
>
> (c) The likely effect of any order, or of any decision by the Court not to exercise its powers under subsection (3), on the health, safety, or well-being of the parties and of any relevant child; and
>
> (d) The conduct of the parties in relation to each other and otherwise.

Applicants should provide a clear statement addressing each criteria under section 33(6) and append relevant documentary evidence to support the statement. In the case of a respondent, they should provide a statement in response with supporting documentation where available. The following points are useful to have in mind in these applications. In respect of housing needs and housing resources, the parties should also set out what their housing needs are, including the number of rooms, location, and if there are alternatives accommodation available for either party, this should be stated. Examples of alternative accommodation can include a room with a family member. Consideration should obviously be given to the children's housing needs, including if the property in question has been specifically adapted for the child, this may be a reason why the child needs to remain in the property. This limb is particularly important in cases where an applicant is seeking an occupation order requiring the respondent to vacate the property, as the court will be anxious to avoid a party being homeless. Parties should provide property particulars to support their case where are available.

The financial resources of each of the parties includes savings, income etc. Parties should state what financial resources they hold including whether they have sufficient financial resources to afford alternative accommodation. This is particularly important in cases where the respondent also has financial obligations towards the property and may now have further financial obligations such as rent and other outgoings on the alternative accommodation. The likely effect on the health, safety, or wellbeing of the parties and of any relevant child, if an occupation order being made or refused should be clearly set out. In terms of the conduct of the parties, if there has been domestic abuse or other unwanted behaviour which makes continued occupation of the respondent untenable, this should be referred to.

## 3.3    Section 35 – Occupation Orders

This section should be used where a former spouse or civil partner with no existing right to occupy the property wishes to apply for an occupation order. For an occupation order under this section, there are three conditions that must be satisfied. The first is that the applicant must be a former spouse or civil partner who has no existing right to occupy. This can include an applicant who has recently finalised an international divorce, and up until the decree absolute was pronounced, the applicant had matrimonial home rights giving them the right to occupy the home in England. Second, the respondent is entitled to occupy the property. Finally, the property was, or was intended to be, their home. When establishing the final condition, it is useful to provide any evidence showing that the property was intended to be a home, particularly in instances where the respondent is likely to challenge this point.

An occupation order under this section must contain a declaration pursuant to section 35(3) or (4) as appropriate. This should be borne in mind when making an application and crucially in drafting orders. Where the applicant is in occupation of the property, the occupation order must contain a provision which gives the applicant the right not to be evicted, or excluded from the property, or any part of it by the respondent for the duration specified in the order, and prohibiting the respondent from evicting or excluded the applicant during the same period. This is very important as without such a provision, the respondent has the right to evict the applicant, or instruct a third party to do so on their behalf. If the applicant does not occupy the property, the occupation order must contain a declaratory provision giving the applicant the right to enter and occupy the property for the duration of the order, and to require the respondent to permit the exercise of that right.

In deciding whether to make an occupation order under this provision, which contains either of the declaratory provisions above, the court shall have regard to all the circumstances including the factors set out in section 35(6) which are as follows:

(a) the housing needs and housing resources of each of the parties and of any relevant child;

(b) the financial resources of each of the parties;

(c) the likely effect of any order, or of any decision by the court not to exercise its powers by including declaratory provisions in the order, on the health, safety, or well-being of the parties and of any relevant child;

(d) the conduct of the parties in relation to each other and otherwise;

(e) the length of time that has elapsed since the parties ceased to live together;

(f) the length of time that has elapsed since the marriage or civil partnership was dissolved or annulled; and

(g) the existence of any pending proceedings between the parties—

  i. for an order under section 23A or 24 of the Matrimonial Causes Act 1973 (property adjustment orders in connection with divorce proceedings etc.);

  ii. for a property adjustment order under Part 2 of Schedule 5 to the Civil Partnership Act 2004;

  iii. for an order under paragraph 1(2)(d) or (e) of Schedule 1 to the Children Act 1989 (orders for financial relief against parents); or

  iv. relating to the legal or beneficial ownership of the dwelling-house.

The court may also include provisions regulating the occupation of the property under section 35(5). Some of these provisions include regulating the occupation by either or both parties, excluding the respondent from a defined area in which the property is included etc. In determining whether to include one or more of these provisions, and if so, in what manner, the court should have regard to all the circumstances of the case included in (a) to (e) above.

The court also has to consider the balance of harm test under section 35(8), which is different from that under section 33(7). In order for the balance of harm test to apply, the court must first decide to make an occupation order but is then required to 'include a subsection 5 provision, if not doing so would cause greater harm attributable to the respondent's conduct than doing so. Unlike section 33 orders, section 35 occupation orders can only be made for a specified period not exceeding 6 months. These orders can be extended on one or more occasions for a maximum of 6 months each time.

## 3.4 Occupation Orders – section 36 FLA 1996

This section only applies to cohabitants and former cohabitants who are not entitled to occupy, which is a requirement to make a proper application under this section. Like the other provisions, the respondent should be a cohabitant or former cohabitant who is entitled to occupy the property, and the property in question is the home in which the parties live, did live or intended to live.[28] If the court makes an occupation order under section 36, where the applicant is not occupying the home, the occupation order must contain a provision under section 36(4), giving the applicant the right to enter into and occupy the property for the period specified in the

---

[28] FLA 1996, section 36(1).

order, and require the respondent to permit the applicant exercise that right. If the applicant is occupying the property, it must contain provisions under section 36(3), giving the applicant the right not to be evicted by the respondent from the property or any part of it, and for the respondent to permit the applicant to exercise this right. These orders can be made for a period not exceeding 6 months, but this period may be extended on one occasion for a further period not exceeding 6 months.

An occupation order under this section may also contain discretionary provisions under section subsection 5, which includes a provision requiring the respondent to leave the property. In deciding whether an order should contain one of the discretionary provisions under subsection 5, the court shall consider all the circumstances of the case including the factors that mirror section 33(7)(a) to (d) and, whether not including a provision under subsection 5 would cause greater harm to the applicant and/or relevant child attributable to the respondent's conduct than doing so. The latter part is the balance of harm test which is set out in section 36(8).

## 3.5 Power of Arrest and Occupation Orders

There is no inherent power to attach a power of arrest. Section 47 provides that if a court makes an occupation order, and it appears to the court that the respondent has used or threatened violence against the applicant or a relevant child, the court shall attach a power of arrest to one or more of the provisions, unless satisfied that in all the circumstances of the case the applicant or child will be adequately protected without such a power of arrest.[29]

---

[29] Family Law Act 1996, section 47(2).

A power of arrest can be attached to an occupation order made without notice to the respondent. For this to apply, the court must be satisfied that the respondent has used or threatened violence and that there is a risk of significant harm if a power of arrest is not attached.[30] The power of arrest must be announced in open court. If a power of arrest is attached to the occupation order the clauses to which the power is attached must be set out in Form FL406. A penal notice, warning of the consequences of disobedience, must appear on the face of every injunction. In the case of an occupation order, the penal notice is in the standard form. Section 47(4) enables the court when attaching a power of arrest to a without notice order to provide that the power of arrest is to have effect for a shorter period than the other provisions of the order. This provision is rarely used although the Court of Appeal has held that this permits a similar order in the case of final orders (*Re B-J (Power of Arrest)* [2000] 2 FLR 443, CA).

As already mentioned, a power of arrest does not need to be attached to a non-molestation order as breaching this order is a criminal offence. The power of arrest authorises a police officer to arrest, without warrant, a person whom the officer has reasonable cause for suspecting is in breach of any part of an order to which the power attaches.[31] Once the court makes an occupation order with a power of arrest attached, it is important that the respondent is served personally, without delay.

---

[30] Family Law Act 1996, section 47(3).

[31] Family Law Act 1996, section 47(6).

## 3.6 Additional Orders – Provisions for repairs and payment of outgoings

When the court makes an occupation order under either section 33, 35 or 36 of the FLA 1996, it also has the power, either when the order is made or at any time thereafter, to make an additional order imposing additional obligations on either party. Additional orders cannot be attached to an occupation order under section 37 or 38 of the FLA 1996. These additional orders are made under section 40 of the FLA 1996, which allows the court to:

(a) Impose obligations on either party to repair and maintain the home or to take responsibility for the mortgage, rent and other outgoings.

(b) Order that the partner occupying the home or any part of it to make periodical payments to the other party in respect of the home if the other party would have been entitled to occupy the home by virtue of their interest in the property. These payments are also known as occupation rent and are intended to be a form of compensation for the loss of the right to occupy the home.

(c) Make orders granting either party possession or use of furniture or other contents of the home, and to take reasonable care of any furniture or other contents of the home.

(d) Order that either party takes reasonable steps to keep the home and any furniture or other contents secure.

Additional orders cannot last longer than the occupation order itself. Practically, applying for additional provision under section 40 may sometimes be better and quicker than making a separate application for maintenance pending suit. On the face of it, section 40 may seem useful as a means of receiving financial provision from one party. However, a key limitation with section 40 is that there is no procedure for enforcing compliance. In *Nwogbe v Nwogbe* [2000] 2 FLR 744, CA Butler-Sloss P stated that 'it was clear that orders under section 40... were unenforceable and of no value to the spouse or cohabitee remaining in occupation. That was a serious omission which required urgent alteration'. It follows that if a party fails to make payments as ordered these cannot be enforce. In comparison, financial provision can be made in the interim under the MCA 1973, which can be enforced.

When making applications for additional orders for payments of outgoings, applicants should fully address their own financial position to demonstrate to the court why they are unable to afford the payments. The respondent should provide documentary evidence regarding affordability on their part, and to show the court that the applicant is able to meet the payments sought.

# CHAPTER FOUR

# WITHOUT NOTICE (EX PARTE) APPLICATIONS

Without notice applications, also known as ex parte applications, are provided under section 45 of the FLA 1996. It is commonly the case that applicants may seek to make an application for a non-molestation order and/or occupation order without notice to the respondent in circumstances which so justify. Section 45 provides that the court may only make a without notice order where it is 'just and convenient' to do so. In determining whether to exercise its powers to make an ex parte order, the court shall have regard to all the circumstances of the case. This includes any risk of significant harm to the applicant or child attributable to the respondent's conduct if an order is not made immediately, whether it is likely that the applicant will be deterred or prevented from pursuing the application if an order is not made immediately, and whether there is reason to believe that the respondent is aware of the proceedings but is deliberately evading service and the applicant or child will be seriously prejudiced by the delay involved in effecting substituted service.[32]

---

[32] Family Law Act 1996, s 45(2).

## 4.1 Guidance from case law

The correct approach to without notice applications was recently considered by Mrs Justice Lieven in *DS v AC* [2023] EWFC 46. Lieven J said at [24]:

> It is important that these principles are applied properly, and orders are not simply granted by default. In particular, it is important for all concerned to note that a without notice application should only be made in exceptional circumstances where there is a risk of significant harm. If a without notice application is made, then the statement in support must expressly deal with why the case is exceptional and what the significant risk alleged is. There can be no doubt that far too many such applications are made where there is no reasonable basis to grant the application without notice.

In this case, Lieven J concluded that the earlier judge had been correct to refuse to make a non-molestation order without notice to the respondent in circumstances where there had been no contact from the respondent before the application was made.[33] Given the gap in time, it was wholly inappropriate on those facts for an ex parte order should have been made. There must be a level of urgency, which justifies an application for a non-molestation order being made ex parte. Often applications for a non-molestation order are made that contain allegations that are quite historic. From experience, allegations that are relied upon that have happened a few months ago are unlikely to be sufficient to persuade a court that an order should be made on an ex parte basis. Based on this, before applying for an ex parte order, the applicant should carefully consider and set out why they say they

---

[33] [2023] EWFC 46, [25].

are at risk of significant harm and an order is required without notice to the respondent. The timing of the conduct complained of should be recent, and where such conduct has ceased, it is likely that the court will take the view that the intervention of the court is not required to control the respondent's behaviour. Other instances which have been found to justify an ex parte order include where the respondent's bail conditions are coming to an end and the behaviour complained of is ongoing or remains a concern.

The courts are quite strict about notice in some circumstances. If an application is made 2-3 weeks after the 'most recent' incident, and in between that time, nothing has been done by the applicant, they are likely to struggle to persuade the court that a protective order is needed without notice to the respondent. The court may say the application is not suited without notice and list the application on notice. Notice should be given where it is safe to do so. There are clearly circumstances where it is not safe to give notice. An obvious example is where giving notice to the respondent of an application may prevent the applicant from bringing the application or further harm may befall the applicant.

When orders are made on an ex parte basis, the order should be for a defined period. Although there is no requirement for the order to be limited in time, the practice is that such orders are usually time-limited and indeed should be. This can be for either 6 months or 12 month unless varied or discharged at an earlier date by the court. Parties and their representatives should confirm the maximum duration for orders as defined in the statute, as making orders without notice foes not alter the position.

Whilst the Court has the power to make a non-molestation order or occupation order without notice to the respondent, it is commonly the case that the court will be more willing to make a non-molestation order on a without notice basis as opposed to an occupation order. This is because a respondent has no legal right to undergo the actions prohibited by a non-molestation order, such as inflicting or threatening violence, or damaging property owned by the applicant or relevant child. The commentary in the Red Book in respect of section 45 of the FLA 1996 explains that making a non-molestation order which such provisions without notice to the respondent do not infringe his or her legal rights as they have no legal right to inflict injury or threaten violence. The same cannot be said about an occupation order which has the effect of depriving the respondent from their home or limiting their use of the home.

In contrast to non-molestation orders, an occupation order overrides the proprietary rights of the respondent. However, they do not extinguish proprietary rights. In *G v G (Ouster: Ex part application)* [1990] 1 FLR 395, CA and *Masich v Masich* (1977) Fam Law 245 CA, it was said that exclusion orders should seldom be granted on a without notice basis. Similar reasoning applies to occupation orders. It follows that although the court has the power to grant an occupation order on a without notice basis, it will only do so in exceptional circumstances. From experience, at an urgent hearing where both orders are sought, it is commonly the case that a non-molestation order is made without notice, and the application for an occupation orders is listed to be reheard at a return date or later directions hearing on notice. This gives the respondent an opportunity to put their case on the application and understand the likely effect on the respondent if an occupation order is made.

## 4.2   Practical tips – The Application and Statements

Practically, applicants would be required to provide a statement containing allegations of domestic abuse that the court can rely upon to make an order, based on what is being alleged, without needing to question whether something has occurred from the other side. This is the whole basis of an ex parte application – i.e., they are granted on the strength of what the applicant says. Ex parte occupation orders do not happen very often. From experience, even where an applicant requests that this be listed without notice, the court tends to assess the reasons for the without notice application, and if the court is not satisfied that the reasons are sufficient, the application for the occupation order is listed on notice. There are occasions where a non-molestation order has been made, which is tantamount to an occupation order. This tends to be where a zonal clause is added such as "the respondent must not go 100 metres of the family home" or going on to a particular road. A non-molestation order with a zonal clause tends to be more frequent.

The circumstances that justify such a non-molestation order with a zonal clause, include where the respondent is not living in the same property as the applicant, the respondent clearly has somewhere else to go (the applicant should evidence this, which on an ex parte can be difficult) or there is some other compelling reason why a zonal clause is needed. A zonal clause for children's school and workplace are more common as respondents do not need to attend these places and can be less restrictive. However, clauses prohibiting the respondent from going to their home can be very restrictive.

Statements should be made as clear as possible. Applicants commonly use pro forma statements. They can be useful for some, but it is not necessarily sufficient. As much detail is needed as possible. If there is text message evidence, these should be attached to demonstrate the allegations the applicant says have taken place. Anything to further assist you should be used. For example, screenshots of text or WhatsApp messages, call logs if allegations of harassment are raised etc. Ultimately, what is required is a concrete statement setting out what allegations are being relied upon, dates of allegations, what evidence there is, whether there are any witnesses. A statement should also identify if any third-party agencies have been informed such as the police, GP, social services, or domestic abuse charities as this can affect what directions, if any, are made at a later stage. Applicants and the lawyers representing them should have in mind that this may be the applicant's last statement, or evidence at the final hearing. Therefore, it is important to give the first statement your best shot as much as possible.

## 4.3  Duties that attach to ex parte applications

It is important that when making an ex parte application, an applicant ensures that they come to the court with clean hands. This is because where no notice, or short notice is given, the applicant is fixed with a high duty of candour. In *Re S (Ex parte Orders)* [2001] FLR 308 it was stated that:

> Those who seek relief ex parte are under a duty to make the fullest and most candid and frank disclosure of all the relevant circumstances known to them. This duty is not confined to the material facts: it extends to all relevant matters, whether of fact or of law. The principle is as applicable in the Family Division as elsewhere. Those who fail in this duty, and those who misrepresent matters to the court, expose themselves to the very real risk of being denied interlocutory relief whether or not they have a good arguable case or even a strong prima facie case.

Therefore, everything in the statement should be accurate and honest. Where matters do not assist your case, this should be raised, particularly in an *ex parte* application where the other side is not present. Legal representatives should be aware of their professional obligations including not to mislead the court knowingly or inadvertently. In essence, ensure that the full picture is presented. Also, when taking instructions from an applicant and giving them their options, lawyers should undertake sufficient research into anything that may assist or undermine their case.

When making ex parte applications, applicants and their representatives should keep in mind the principles and safeguards to be observed on an application for an *ex parte* freezing or search order as found in *L v K (Freezing Orders: Principles and Safeguards)* [2013] EWHC 1735 (Fam). One of the principles is that lawyers should have a note of what happened in the without notice hearing, and this note must be sent to the respondent who is subject to any orders made. Unfortunately, this safeguard is not always complied with in practice, and it seems to be something individuals ignore. A note of the hearing should be taken and given to the respondent, so s/he is aware of what exactly was said, as counsel or the representative, is very likely to have expanded upon the information in the supporting statement. A note can be invaluable at a return date, as without paying for a transcript, a respondent may not know what was said. The aim is to provide as much visibility as possible.

Finally, the following should be borne in mind when drafting ex parte orders. The order must clear spell out that (a) it was made in the absence of the respondent and that the court has considered only the evidence of the applicant and (b) the court has made no finding of fact. Where the evidence is written, it must be identified in the order. Where, exceptionally, the court has received oral or other evidence (e.g., a photograph) that evidence should be recorded on the face of

NON-MOLESTATION ORDERS AND OCCUPATION ORDERS IN FAMILY PROCEEDINGS

the order or reduced to writing and served with the order. On 14 July 2023, the President of the Family Division issued practice guidance to address some of the practical and procedural aspects of applications under section 42 of the Family Law Act 1996, known as non-molestation injunctions.[34] Readers are directed to the *Practice Guidance: Non-molestation Injunctions under the Family Law Act 1996* which replaces the guidance previously issued on 18 January 2017.

The recent guidance states that an order made without notice must contain a statement of the right to make an application to set aside or vary the order under FPR 2010, rule 18.11.[35] This requirement is not satisfied by the phrase 'liberty to apply'. Rather, the order must clearly state that the respondent is entitled, without waiting for the return day, to apply to set aside or vary the order. If an application is made to set aside or vary the order, the court must list the application as a matter of urgency, within a matter of days at most. In all cases, where an ex parte order is made, section 45(3) of the FLA 1996 requires that the respondent has an opportunity to make representations relating to the order as just and convenient at a full hearing. This hearing is known as the 'return date'.

## 4.4  Return Date

The return date is aimed at ensuring fairness and is the first time that the respondent will have an opportunity to make representations to the court. At the return date, the court reconsiders the application and whether the orders should continue. The President's Guidance on

---

[34] Sir Andrew McFarlane The President of the Family Division, *Practice Guidance: Non-molestation Injunctions under the Family Law Act 1996* issued on 14 July 2023.

[35] Family Procedure Rules 2010, r18.10(3).

injunctions provides that the return date should ideally be listed within 14 days, however, volume of work within the courts may mean that 28 days is all that can be achieved.[36] A return date may be in person or remotely. In terms of listing and allocation, the guidance states that it is not necessary for the return date to come back before the same level of judge that made the *ex parte* order. What is important is fixing the return date and this return hearing must be specified in the order, or the hearing notice sent alongside it. It is not an adequate substitute for the respondent to be given the permission to apply for a hearing date.[37]

It can be helpful for the respondent to file and serve a statement responding to the application and the applicant's statement ahead of the return date, if possible. The statement should append any relevant supporting documentation. This allows the court and the other side to know the respondent's position, and potentially consider whether there is scope for compromising the applications by way of undertakings, cross-undertakings or the orders continuing on the basis of no findings of fact and no admissions being made. If the applications cannot be compromised at the return date, the application(s) will need to be case managed and listed for a contested final hearing.

---

[36] Sir Andrew McFarlane The President of the Family Division, *Practice Guidance: Non-molestation Injunctions under the Family Law Act 1996* issued on 14 July 2023, para 9.

[37] ibid, para 10.

## 4.5 Case management

Often, the parties' evidence contains reference to the involvement of third parties. This may be police callouts, ambulance callouts, visits to the GP, counsellor, reports from school and so on. Determining which third party disclosure orders are required depends on the evidence and case. Separate disclosure orders should be drawn from the non-molestation order or occupation order.

It is well known that domestic abuse can and often does continue well beyond the point of relationship breakdown. Commonly parties to Family Law Act proceedings are in Children Act proceedings or one party is about to initiate such proceedings. Depending on the stage at which the parties are in Children Act proceedings, parties and their representatives may wish to consider whether the Family Law Act proceedings should be consolidated with the children matter. This can be appropriate where the allegations are the same or similar. This approach is consistent with practice guidance from the President in para 27 which states:

> Courts should put in place a system for identifying parallel proceedings under the FLA and private law proceedings under the Children Act 1989 where allegations of abuse are made between the same parties and should aim to have at least one case management hearing bringing together the two sets of proceedings at an early stage. The court should avoid duplication, and factual findings and evidence should normally be disclosed from one set of proceedings into the other. Courts considering PD12J will have regard to any factual matrix that has already been the subject of determination in FLA proceedings when deciding whether further fact finding in children proceedings is necessary.

Practitioners should have this in mind. There are occasions where private children proceedings have not been commenced or an application has been made but a hearing is yet to be listed, and the FLA matter is being heard at the return date. If it is unclear whether the allegations will be relevant and parties are unsure about consolidation, it can be useful to include a recital on the face of the order relating to this. An example may be as follows 'The applicant/respondent has made an application in the Children Act 1989 with respect to the arrangements for the child/children. It is recorded that today the parties discussed the prospects of consolidating these proceedings with anticipated Children Act proceedings. It was agreed that this shall be a decision for the Judge at the FHDRA in the Children Act proceedings'.

# CHAPTER FIVE

# UNDERTAKINGS

An undertaking is a formal promise by the giver to the court, and not to the other party, that they shall adhere to the terms of the undertaking given to the court.[38] Undertakings should be considered as a way to compromise an application for a non-molestation order or occupation order. Certainly, a respondent may be more willing to offer an undertaking in lieu of a non-molestation order. The court may accept an undertaking from any party to the proceedings in any case where the court has the power to make an occupation order or non-molestation order.[39]

A power of arrest cannot be attached to an undertaking.[40] However, where an undertaking is breached it can be enforced as if it were a non-molestation order or an occupation order in terms corresponding to those of the undertaking. Breach of an undertaking is a contempt of court punishable by way of committal proceedings under Part 37 of the Family Procedure Rules 2010. Any committal application should provide the date and terms of any undertaking alleged breached, and confirmation of the applicant's belief that the respondent understood the terms and consequences of failure to comply with the undertaking.[41]

---

[38] Family Law Act 1996, section 46.

[39] Family Law Act 1996, section 46(1).

[40] Family Law Act 1996, section 46(2).

[41] Family Procedure Rules 2010, r 37.4(2)(f) and (g).

## 5.1 When will the court not accept an undertaking?

The court will not accept an undertaking by a respondent instead of making a non-molestation order in any case where it appears to the court that the respondent has used or threatened violence against the applicant or relevant child, and it is necessary to make an order for their protection so that any breach can be punishable as a criminal offence.[42] The court shall not accept an undertaking instead of making an occupation order where a power of arrest would otherwise be attached to the order.

The issue of undertakings is frequently brought up at a return date where a non-molestation order or an occupation order is made. In considering whether to accept undertakings, applicants and/or their representatives should carefully consider whether an undertaking sufficiently protects an applicant or the child in light of the allegations raised. If there are allegations of physical violence, then an undertaking should not be considered or accepted. The court may also wish to reflect on whether a respondent has previously breached an undertaking as this could indicate that they cannot be trusted to maintain this.

## 5.2 Undertakings from respondents aged less than 18 or lacking capacity

Chapter 2 considered the appropriateness of granting an injunction against respondents who are minors under 18 and/or those who lack capacity, and it was noted that this would not be appropriate. The position regarding undertakings is like unto injunctions. Breach of an undertaking is a contempt of court. Indeed, the Form N117 contains

---

[42] Family Law Act 1996, section 46(3A).

an important notice which states 'if you do not comply with your promises to the court, you may be held to be in contempt of court and imprisoned or fined, or your assets may be seized'. Given the analysis of the authorities discussed in Chapter 2, it can be said that the court does not have the jurisdiction, to accept an undertaking from a minor under 18. This is because of their age and that undertakings would require a penal notice being attached. Also, enforcement of the undertaking is through the same manner of an injunction. From experience where this has occurred, the court chose to accept promises, rather than a formal undertaking, from the minors, which were then recorded on the face of the order. Similarly, an undertaking may be considered inappropriate against a party that lacks capacity as they may not understand the promises that are being offered.

## 5.3 Procedural points in connection with undertakings

The following procedural points should be carefully considered in connection with undertakings. The undertaking should be recorded in Form N117, and the terms should be explained to the respondent by the judge, and the respondent asked to sign the form. Prior to this, a party's legal representative should explain to a party what undertakings are and the consequences of breaching an undertaking. Judges will commonly ask the respondent if this has been explained to them. There are occasions where both parties are providing undertakings. This is formally known as 'cross-undertakings'. The terms given by both parties may be the same or different. Whatever the position, both parties' undertakings must be recorded on separate forms. Once the forms are signed, a copy of the undertaking should be given to both parties before they leave the court building. The Red Book notes that court clerk must record on the back of the Form N117 the way in which service of the undertaking forms have been effected on the respondent.

When undertakings are given, the judge has the following responsibilities. The judge should approve the terms of the proposed promises and ensure that the giver understands what has been promised and the consequences of the breach. The judge should also consider whether the signature of the giver should be included in the box on the back of the form to avoid dispute about what happened when the undertaking was given. In practice, it is rare for undertakings to be taken in the absence of the giver. However, if this is done, advocates should have clear instructions on this and ensure that the giver understands the consequences of breaching the undertaking.

# CHAPTER SIX

# PROCEDURAL GUIDANCE: APPLICATIONS FOR NON-MOLESTATION ORDERS AND OCCUPATION ORDERS

The procedural requirements for applications under Part IV of the Family Law Act 1996 are set out in Part 10 of the Family Procedure Rules 2010.

## 6.1　Making an application

The relevant application form for an occupation order or a non-molestation order is Form FL401. The proceedings can be commenced either by way of a free-standing application or within existing proceedings. The application must be supported by a witness statement. The application form should be supported by a witness statement. The statement must clear set out which section the application is being brought under (i.e., under section 33 or 36), and how the legal test is established, or how the parties are associated persons. The supporting statement can be incorporated within the application form. An application to vary, extend or discharge a non-molestation order or occupation order is made on Form FL403. The same rules as to the requirement for a supporting statement, filling in Form C8 if required, service and representations by a mortgagee or landlord apply.

Where an application is made on an ex parte basis, the witness statement must address the reasons why notice has not been given. In doing so, reference should be made to the criteria provided in section 45 of the FLA 1996. Providing the reasons why the application is made without notice is important so that the respondent knows why the application was made, and to persuade the court to make the order without notice to the respondent. The witness statement must contain a statement of truth, as required under FPR 2010 r 17.2(1)(b).

Proceedings may be commenced in the High Court, or the Family Court. However, in practice this is usually always done in the Family Court. If the applicant does not wish to reveal their address or that of a relevant child, a Form C8 should be completed. Doing this gives notice to the court of the address and those details will not be disclosed to the any other party unless the court directs otherwise. The completed Form C8 is then sealed and placed on the court file.

## 6.2   Service of the application and order on the respondent

In an application made on notice the applicant must serve on the respondent a copy of the application and any supporting witness statement and a notice of hearing or directions appointment listed by the court. FPR 2010, Part 6 deals with service of the application. The various modes of service are provided in FPR 2010, r 6.23 which include personal service, first class post, leaving documents at a specified place, fax, or email.

FPR 2010, r 10.3 provides that the application and other documents specified above must be served personally on the respondent not less than two days before the hearing or within such period as the court may direct, unless an order has been made for alternative service under

## APPLICATIONS FOR NON-MOLESTATION ORDERS AND OCCUPATION ORDERS

FPR 2010, r 6.35 or service is dispensed with under r 6.36. Personal service is not essential, but it can be helpful in these cases as the orders take effect once the respondent is made aware of the terms. Personal service is commonly effected by a process server. If the applicant is a litigant in person, the applicant can request the court officer to serve the application on the respondent.[43]

There are occasions where the prescribed methods of service under FPR 2010, r 6.23 are impracticable. This may be because the respondent is unreachable. In such circumstances, the court may direct that steps already taken to bring the application to the respondent's attention amount to good service by way of retrospective service as per FPR 2010, r 6.19(2). Alternatively, the court may give further directions specifying the mode or place of service; the date on which the application is deemed served; and the time for filing an acknowledgment of service or answer.[44] In such occasions, alternative modes of service can include service via text message, WhatsApp[45], Facebook, or via a friend or relative.[46]

In instances where the respondent is present at court when either a non-molestation order and/or occupation order is made, it may be useful to record that personal service is dispensed with. This is an option where the terms of the non-molestation order (and occupation order) have been read out in court and the respondent is aware of the same.

---

[43] Family Procedure Rules 2010, r 10.3(2).

[44] Family Procedure Rules 2010, r 6.19.

[45] *Gray v Hurley* [2020] 1 FLR 182

[46] *HC v FW (Financial Remedies: Assessment of General and Special Needs)* [2018] 2 FLR 70, FD.

Where an applicant applies for an occupation order under section 33, 35 or 36 of FLA 1996, they must serve a copy of the application and notice of the right to make representations in writing or orally on the mortgagee, housing association, or any landlord of the property in question. Once the application has been served, the applicant must serve a certificate of service using Form FL415 as prescribed by FPR 2010, Part 5.

Finally, where an order is made the applicant must as soon as reasonably practicable serve on the respondent personally a copy of the order, and where the order is made without notice, a copy of the application along with the supporting statement, and a copy of the lay justice's written reasons (where the application is heard by Magistrates).[47] The rules make clear that the applicant must not serve the documents listed in the preceding sentence personally on the respondent.

## 6.3   Service of the order on the Police

The police need to be aware of relevant orders, especially where breaching a non-molestation order is a criminal offence and they are likely to be contacted by an applicant if a breach occurs. Where the court makes a non-molestation order or an occupation order with a power of arrest attached, a copy of these orders must be served to 'the officer for the time being in charge of the police station for the applicant's address, or such other police station for the as the court may specify'.[48] When the order is served on the police officer, a statement showing that the respondent has been served with the order

---

[47]   Family Procedure Rules 2010, r 10.6(1).

[48]   Family Procedure Rules 2010, r 10.10(1).

APPLICATIONS FOR NON-MOLESTATION ORDERS AND OCCUPATION ORDERS

or informed of its terms must accompany the same.[49] Service of this documentation must be undertaken by the applicant or the court officer if the applicant is a litigant in person and requests the courts assistance, or the court made the orders on its own initiative.[50] Where an order is made varying or discharging a provision of a non-molestation order or occupation order that has a power of arrest attached, FPR, r10.10(5) requires that the court officer immediately informs the police officer who received a copy of the order (and the officer if the applicant's address has changed) and deliver a copy of the varied or discharged order.

## 6.4 Vulnerable persons and Special measures

The quality of evidence of a party or witness that raises allegations of domestic abuse may be affected without certain measure being put in place to allow them to provide complete, coherent, and accurate evidence. In this context, FPR 2010 rule 3A.1 defines 'coherence' as referring to 'a witnesses' or a party's ability in giving evidence to give answers which address the questions put to the witness or the party and which can be understood both individually and collectively'. To address this, the family court has the power to make 'participation directions' to assist a person during proceedings, which can include a direction that a particular measure should be made available. These measures are known as 'special measures'.

Special measures are a series of directions aimed at helping a party or witness in proceedings participate or give evidence in court proceedings in circumstances where it appears to the court that the

---

[49] Family Procedure Rules 2010, r 10.10(2).

[50] Family Procedure Rules 2010, r 10.10(3) and r 10.6(2).

quality of their evidence would be diminished if such measures were not available. Examples of these range of special measures include permitting them to give evidence from behind a screen or via a live link, providing them with the assistance of an intermediary. When either representing an applicant for a Family Law Act application or representing a respondent, it is important for both advocates to have at the forefront of their mind the need for any special measures.

In *Re S (Vulnerable Party: Fairness of Proceedings)* [2022] EWCA Civ 8, Lord Justice Baker stated that it is the duty of the court (which also extends to legal representatives) to identify any party or witness who is a vulnerable person at the earliest possible stage of any family proceedings, and 'to ensure that each party or witness can participate in proceedings without the quality of their evidence being diminished'.[51] This is confirmed in rules 1.1(2), 1.2 and 1.4 and Part 3A FPR 2010.

Section 65 of the Domestic Abuse Act 2021 ('DAA 2021'), which came into force on 21 July 2022, prohibits alleged perpetrators of domestic abuse from directly cross-examining victims of domestic abuse in family proceedings. The section also prohibits an alleged victim of domestic abuse from cross-examining an alleged preparator. It should be noted that, the DAA 2021 refers to there being either a conviction, caution, injunction, or specific evidence of domestic abuse. However, the court has a discretion to apply section 65 if it appears to it that the quality of evidence given by the party or witness is likely to be diminished if the cross-examination (or continued cross-examination) is conducted by the party in person and would be likely to be improved if a participation direction were given.

---

[51] Para 39.

# CONCLUDING REMAKRS

Civil remedies are an important component of the legal response to victims of domestic abuse as the two main remedies under the Family Law Act 1996 provide victims with a remedy that is accessible to them at their own initiative. This is particularly welcoming where there are an increasing number of litigants in person, who may require the urgent protection of the courts. It is hoped that this guidance can be of great assistance to those who may find themselves making or resisting applications under the Act, as well as the professionals who may be instructed to represent parties in these cases.

# MORE BOOKS BY LAW BRIEF PUBLISHING

A selection of our other titles available now:-

| |
|---|
| 'A Practical Guide to the Independent School Standards – September 2023 Edition' by Sarah McKimm |
| 'A Practical Guide to Estate Administration and Crypto Assets' by Richard Marshall |
| 'A Practical Guide to Managing GDPR Data Subject Access Requests – Second Edition' by Patrick O'Kane |
| 'A Practical Guide to Parental Alienation in Private and Public Law Children Cases' by Sam King QC & Frankie Shama |
| 'Contested Heritage – Removing Art from Land and Historic Buildings' by Richard Harwood QC, Catherine Dobson, David Sawtell |
| 'The Limits of Separate Legal Personality: When Those Running a Company Can Be Held Personally Liable for Losses Caused to Third Parties Outside of the Company' by Dr Mike Wilkinson |
| 'A Practical Guide to Transgender Law' by Robin Moira White & Nicola Newbegin |
| 'A Practical Guide to 'Stranded Spouses' in Family Law' by Mani Singh Basi |
| 'A Practical Guide to Residential Freehold Conveyancing' by Lorraine Richardson |
| 'A Practical Guide to Pensions on Divorce for Lawyers' by Bryan Scant |
| 'A Practical Guide to Challenging Sham Marriage Allegations in Immigration Law' by Priya Solanki |
| 'A Practical Guide to Digital Communications Evidence in Criminal Law' by Sam Willis |
| 'A Practical Guide to Legal Rights in Scotland' by Sarah-Jane Macdonald |
| 'A Practical Guide to New Build Conveyancing' by Paul Sams & Rebecca East |
| 'A Practical Guide to Defending Barristers in Disciplinary Cases' by Marc Beaumont |
| 'A Practical Guide to Inherited Wealth on Divorce' by Hayley Trim |
| 'A Practical Guide to Practice Direction 12J and Domestic Abuse in Private Law Children Proceedings' by Rebecca Cross & Malvika Jaganmohan |

| |
|---|
| 'A Practical Guide to Confiscation and Restraint' by Narita Bahra QC, John Carl Townsend, David Winch |
| 'A Practical Guide to the Law of Forests in Scotland' by Philip Buchan |
| 'A Practical Guide to Health and Medical Cases in Immigration Law' by Rebecca Chapman & Miranda Butler |
| 'A Practical Guide to Bad Character Evidence for Criminal Practitioners by Aparna Rao |
| 'A Practical Guide to Extradition Law post-Brexit' by Myles Grandison et al |
| 'A Practical Guide to Hoarding and Mental Health for Housing Lawyers' by Rachel Coyle |
| 'A Practical Guide to Psychiatric Claims in Personal Injury – 2nd Edition' by Liam Ryan |
| 'Stephens on Contractual Indemnities' by Richard Stephens |
| 'A Practical Guide to the EU Succession Regulation' by Richard Frimston |
| 'A Practical Guide to Solicitor and Client Costs – 2nd Edition' by Robin Dunne |
| 'Constructive Dismissal – Practice Pointers and Principles' by Benjimin Burgher |
| 'A Practical Guide to Religion and Belief Discrimination Claims in the Workplace' by Kashif Ali |
| 'A Practical Guide to the Law of Medical Treatment Decisions' by Ben Troke |
| 'Fundamental Dishonesty and QOCS in Personal Injury Proceedings: Law and Practice' by Jake Rowley |
| 'A Practical Guide to the Law in Relation to School Exclusions' by Charlotte Hadfield & Alice de Coverley |
| 'A Practical Guide to Divorce for the Silver Separators' by Karin Walker |
| 'The Right to be Forgotten – The Law and Practical Issues' by Melissa Stock |
| 'A Practical Guide to Planning Law and Rights of Way in National Parks, the Broads and AONBs' by James Maurici QC, James Neill et al |
| 'A Practical Guide to Election Law' by Tom Tabori |
| 'A Practical Guide to the Law in Relation to Surrogacy' by Andrew Powell |
| 'A Practical Guide to Claims Arising from Fatal Accidents – 2nd Edition' by James Patience |
| 'A Practical Guide to the Ownership of Employee Inventions – From Entitlement to Compensation' by James Tumbridge & Ashley Roughton |
| 'A Practical Guide to Asbestos Claims' by Jonathan Owen & Gareth McAloon |

| |
|---|
| 'A Practical Guide to Stamp Duty Land Tax in England and Northern Ireland' by Suzanne O'Hara |
| 'A Practical Guide to the Law of Farming Partnerships' by Philip Whitcomb |
| 'Covid-19, Homeworking and the Law – The Essential Guide to Employment and GDPR Issues' by Forbes Solicitors |
| 'Covid-19 and Criminal Law – The Essential Guide' by Ramya Nagesh |
| 'Covid-19 and Family Law in England and Wales – The Essential Guide' by Safda Mahmood |
| 'A Practical Guide to the Law of Unlawful Eviction and Harassment – 2nd Edition' by Stephanie Lovegrove |
| 'Covid-19, Brexit and the Law of Commercial Leases – The Essential Guide' by Mark Shelton |
| 'A Practical Guide to Costs in Personal Injury Claims – 2nd Edition' by Matthew Hoe |
| 'A Practical Guide to the General Data Protection Regulation (GDPR) – 2$^{nd}$ Edition' by Keith Markham |
| 'Ellis on Credit Hire – Sixth Edition' by Aidan Ellis & Tim Kevan |
| 'A Practical Guide to Working with Litigants in Person and McKenzie Friends in Family Cases' by Stuart Barlow |
| 'Protecting Unregistered Brands: A Practical Guide to the Law of Passing Off' by Lorna Brazell |
| 'A Practical Guide to Secondary Liability and Joint Enterprise Post-Jogee' by Joanne Cecil & James Mehigan |
| 'A Practical Guide to the Pre-Action RTA Claims Protocol for Personal Injury Lawyers' by Antonia Ford |
| 'A Practical Guide to Neighbour Disputes and the Law' by Alexander Walsh |
| 'A Practical Guide to Forfeiture of Leases' by Mark Shelton |
| 'A Practical Guide to Coercive Control for Legal Practitioners and Victims' by Rachel Horman |
| 'A Practical Guide to the Law of Driverless Cars – Second Edition' by Alex Glassbrook, Emma Northey & Scarlett Milligan |
| 'A Practical Guide to TOLATA Claims' by Greg Williams |
| 'A Practical Guide to Elderly Law – 2nd Edition' by Justin Patten |
| 'A Practical Guide to Responding to Housing Disrepair and Unfitness Claims' by Iain Wightwick |

| |
|---|
| 'A Practical Guide to the Law of Bullying and Harassment in the Workplace' by Philip Hyland |
| 'How to Be a Freelance Solicitor: A Practical Guide to the SRA-Regulated Freelance Solicitor Model' by Paul Bennett |
| 'A Practical Guide to Prison Injury Claims' by Malcolm Johnson |
| 'A Practical Guide to the Small Claims Track – 2nd Edition' by Dominic Bright |
| 'A Practical Guide to Advising Clients at the Police Station' by Colin Stephen McKeown-Beaumont |
| 'A Practical Guide to Antisocial Behaviour Injunctions' by Iain Wightwick |
| 'Practical Mediation: A Guide for Mediators, Advocates, Advisers, Lawyers, and Students in Civil, Commercial, Business, Property, Workplace, and Employment Cases' by Jonathan Dingle with John Sephton |
| 'The Mini-Pupillage Workbook' by David Boyle |
| 'A Practical Guide to Crofting Law' by Brian Inkster |
| 'A Practical Guide to the Law of Domain Names and Cybersquatting' by Andrew Clemson |
| 'A Practical Guide to the Law of Gender Pay Gap Reporting' by Harini Iyengar |
| 'NHS Whistleblowing and the Law' by Joseph England |
| 'Employment Law and the Gig Economy' by Nigel Mackay & Annie Powell |
| 'A Practical Guide to Noise Induced Hearing Loss (NIHL) Claims' by Andrew Mckie, Ian Skeate, Gareth McAloon |
| 'An Introduction to Beauty Negligence Claims – A Practical Guide for the Personal Injury Practitioner' by Greg Almond |
| 'Intercompany Agreements for Transfer Pricing Compliance' by Paul Sutton |
| 'Zen and the Art of Mediation' by Martin Plowman |
| 'A Practical Guide to the SRA Principles, Individual and Law Firm Codes of Conduct 2019 – What Every Law Firm Needs to Know' by Paul Bennett |
| 'A Practical Guide to Adoption for Family Lawyers' by Graham Pegg |
| 'A Practical Guide to Industrial Disease Claims' by Andrew Mckie & Ian Skeate |
| 'A Practical Guide to Redundancy' by Philip Hyland |
| 'A Practical Guide to Vicarious Liability' by Mariel Irvine |
| 'A Practical Guide to Applications for Landlord's Consent and Variation of Leases' by Mark Shelton |
| 'A Practical Guide to Relief from Sanctions Post-Mitchell and Denton' by Peter Causton |

| |
|---|
| 'A Practical Guide to Equity Release for Advisors' by Paul Sams |
| 'A Practical Guide to Financial Services Claims' by Chris Hegarty |
| 'The Law of Houses in Multiple Occupation: A Practical Guide to HMO Proceedings' by Julian Hunt |
| 'Occupiers, Highways and Defective Premises Claims: A Practical Guide Post-Jackson – 2nd Edition' by Andrew Mckie |
| 'A Practical Guide to Financial Ombudsman Service Claims' by Adam Temple & Robert Scrivenor |
| 'A Practical Guide to Running Housing Disrepair and Cavity Wall Claims: 2nd Edition' by Andrew Mckie & Ian Skeate |
| 'A Practical Guide to Holiday Sickness Claims – 2nd Edition' by Andrew Mckie & Ian Skeate |
| 'Arguments and Tactics for Personal Injury and Clinical Negligence Claims' by Dorian Williams |
| 'A Practical Guide to Drone Law' by Rufus Ballaster, Andrew Firman, Eleanor Clot |
| 'A Practical Guide to Compliance for Personal Injury Firms Working With Claims Management Companies' by Paul Bennett |
| 'RTA Allegations of Fraud in a Post-Jackson Era: The Handbook – 2nd Edition' by Andrew Mckie |
| 'RTA Personal Injury Claims: A Practical Guide Post-Jackson' by Andrew Mckie |
| 'On Experts: CPR35 for Lawyers and Experts' by David Boyle |
| 'An Introduction to Personal Injury Law' by David Boyle |

These books and more are available to order online direct from the publisher at www.lawbriefpublishing.com, where you can also read free sample chapters. For any queries, contact us on 0844 587 2383 or mail@lawbriefpublishing.com.

Our books are also usually in stock at www.amazon.co.uk with free next day delivery for Prime members, and at good legal bookshops such as Wildy & Sons.

We are regularly launching new books in our series of practical day-to-day practitioners' guides. Visit our website and join our free newsletter to be kept informed and to receive special offers, free chapters, etc.

You can also follow us on Twitter at www.twitter.com/lawbriefpub.

Printed in Great Britain
by Amazon